NON-BEING AND SOMETHING-NESS

Selections from the comic strip
INSIDE WOODY ALLEN

**Drawn by Stuart Hample
With an Introduction by
R. Buckminster Fuller**

Random House
New York

Library of Congress Cataloging in Publication Data
Allen, Woody.
Non-being and somethingness.
I. Hample, Stuart E. II. Title.
PN6728.I5A4   741.5'973   77-90268
ISBN 0-394-73590-0

Manufactured in the United States of America
2   4   6   8   9   7   5   3
First Edition

Introduction by R. Buckminster Fuller

CAST OF CHARACTERS

TETRU	= Tetrahedron	— Could be Bucky
SUMMA	= Octahedron	— Girl Student
CUM	= Icosahedron	— Boy Student
BIGBANG	= Dodecahedron	— Science Hypoth.
SOLIDSTATE	= Cube	— Science Hypoth.
WOODY	= Woody	— Woody

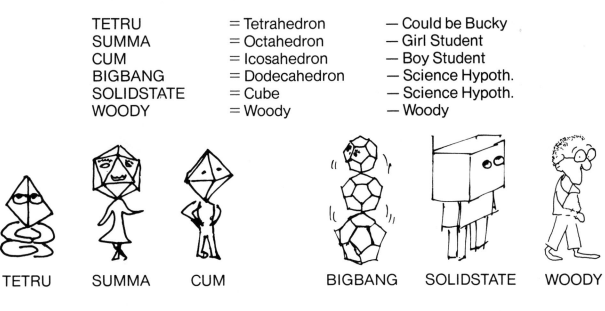

TETRU   SUMMA   CUM   BIGBANG   SOLIDSTATE   WOODY

*Woody's audience gaining
one million per week.
1.000.000 x 50 x 80 =
4,000,000,000 =
4 Billion

⑦

We gave her case the reducio-ad-absurdum from the complex
to the simplex - we'll give you the same treatment but
from the simplex to the complex. OK Solid State--your turn
"Bigbang says she does her great thing with all your little
things. The average human consists of 8 octillion atoms -
written as 8 followed by 28 zeros. Average human beings
of all ages weigh 150 pounds. The largest passenger ship
ever made weighed 85 thousand tons. The largest ocean going
oil tanker fully loaded weighs a million tons.

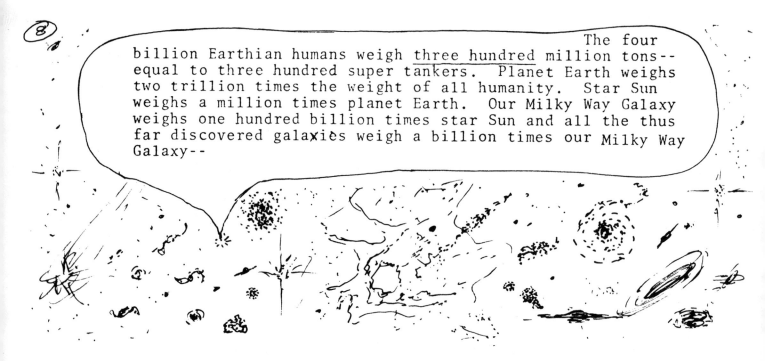

⑧

                                                 The four
billion Earthian humans weigh three hundred million tons--
equal to three hundred super tankers. Planet Earth weighs
two trillion times the weight of all humanity. Star Sun
weighs a million times planet Earth. Our Milky Way Galaxy
weighs one hundred billion times star Sun and all the thus
far discovered galaxies weigh a billion times our Milky Way
Galaxy--

To comprehend scenario universe in conradistinction to the
one frame of a moving picture, for instance a picture of a
it takes many frames to convince us that the butterfly is
of frames to disclose butterflies' interfunctioning with
of frames to elucidate the regenerative interfunctioning
and a thousand generations of human experience historians
and supporting such a phenomenon as humans, their physical
which human minds may deduce, comprehend and employ cosmic
varsity team functioning as local-universe harvesting moni
ever disclose to any one individual what it is all about
eternally regenerative, is the only 100% efficient system
humans to separate individual viewpoints ergo, designs us

BUTTERFLY

Dream or reality, scientific observation and analysis
has proven scenario universe to be an omni-interaccomodative
complex of special case local realizations of a complex
of only mathematically stateable generalized principles,
such as those of leverage, gravity, optics and radiation.
These generalized principles govern all covarying interelation-
ships of all intertransforming systems. These scientific-
ally generalized principles are found to hold true with-
out any exceptions and are therefore inherently eternal.
Ergo, universe has no beginning or ending. Only the local,
always differentiated from one another, individual episodes
of special case, temporal, humanly experiencable manifests
of the generalized principles are terminal. You can
neither comprehend nor express eternity in the special
case terms of temporality.,..

HEY! SOCIAL POWER STRUCTURES - POLITICAL, FINANCIAL.
DID YOU GET THAT? UNIVERSE HAS NO END;
IT CANNOT LONG TOLERATE TREACHEROUS MEANS
AS SEEMINGLY JUSTIFYING VICTORIOUS ENDS

classical "One Big Simultaneous Thing" universe we first note that
caterpillar, does not tell us it is going to become a butterfly and
flying - millions of frames to disclose how the butterfly flies: billions
planet Earth's ecological regeneration of its sentient life; quadrillions
of planet Earth's ecology with cosmic regeneration; quintillions of frames
to piece together the total cosmic strategy's raision-d'etre for evolving
and metaphysical information apprehending and storing organisms from
generalized principles aboard planet Earth, thus to fuffill their cosmic
tors and local universe problem solvers - but no number of frames will
and how come. One thing is clear and that is that the universe, being
and is therefore a magnificent design which deliberately confines we
to be limited and not to be GOD.

SOLID STATE, YOU ARE AN IMPOSTER- A NOTHING MASQUERADING AS A SOMETHING. PHYSICS HAS FOUND NO SOLIDS -- HAS FOUND ONLY WAVES SO SHORT AND REPETITIVELY FREQUENT AS TO FRUSTRATE SENSORIAL PENETRATION BETWEEN THEIR BURSTS AS THESE TRANSPIRE IN PURE PRINCIPLE

16

Solidstate and Bigbang, not only are you both imposters you have no demonstrable structural intergrity. Only triangularly faceted polyhedra hold their shapes. Your cubic and dodecahedronal masquerade costume polyhedra have no triangles. You haven't a triangle to your names. You are both bust before you start. You are nonexistant.

17

WITH THESE COSMIC IMPOSTERS OUT OF THE WAY, LET'S INTRODUCE WOODY ALLEN.

THAT'S WHAT WE'RE HERE FOR ANYWAY. OK stars, galaxies -- GIVE WOODY A BIG HAND!

Woody is the master of ceremonies in what may be the last act of humans on Planet Earth or the first act of Humans in Universe. Human muscle is nothing in the cosmic energy scheme - Human minds are cosmically operative. Humans are included in universe for their mind capability function in support of the integrity of eternally regenerative universe. As of what is known as 1977 human muscle, cunning and guns are in control of human affairs. Two individuals are paid over a million dollars by T.V. producers for punching each others' heads for ten minutes... Earthian humans are going through their final ten year exam as to whether they qualify to continue in universe. If physical power persists, we fail; if mind takes command, we qualify.

NON-BEING AND SOMETHING-NESS

PHILOSOPHY

PSYCHIATRY

...SO, YOU SEE, YOU ARE A UNIQUE INDIVIDUAL. NOW GO OUT AND BE YOURSELF.

FOR A WHILE THERE. I WAS ACTUALLY HAVING AN IDENTITY CRISIS...

RELATIONS WITH WOMEN

MY ONE REGRET IN LIFE— ASIDE FROM THE FACT THAT I AM NOT WARREN BEATTY— IS THAT I'M NOT AN AMOEBA.

"AN AMOEBA JUST SPLITS AND FALLS IN LOVE WITH THE OTHER AMOEBA.

"THEN THEY SPLIT AND FALL IN LOVE AND SO ON, AD INFINITUM.

"MAYBE IF I JUST SPLIT..."

YOU NEVER TAKE ME ANYPLACE!

WE NEVER DO ANYTHING INTERESTING!

ALL YOU EVER DO IS **BROOD**! I THOUGHT YOU'D BE **FUNNY**!!

POP!

I THINK I'LL JUST GO BACK TO REGRETTING I'M NOT WARREN BEATTY.

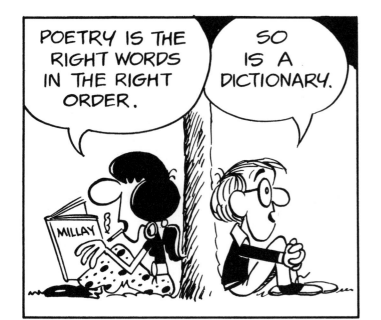

4

FAMILY HISTORY & EARLY CHILDHOOD

5

ARTIST/CELEBRITY

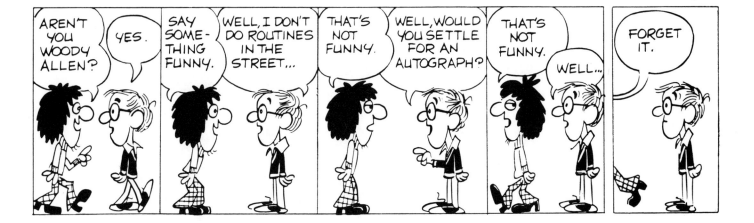

FORCES OF EVIL

"WHEN I'M DRIVING, I MAKE IT A PRACTICE NEVER TO STOP LATE AT NIGHT FOR HITCH-HIKERS.

"BUT SOMETIMES DETERMINATION IS NOT ENOUGH...

"ARMED ONLY WITH A SPORTS CAR AND MY FATAL GOOD LOOKS, I SPEED ALONG A SECLUDED ROAD AT NIGHT...

"A SIX-FOOT-FOUR-INCH HITCH-HIKER WEIGHING 250 LBS. SIGNALS FOR ME TO PICK HIM UP.

"SHREWDLY, I PASS HIM AT 70 M.P.H.

"HE GETS IN."

Afterword

"Inside Woody Allen" is syndicated in newspapers throughout the United States. It also appears in over sixty foreign countries. Here are six examples of how it looks in translation.

ENGLISH

FRENCH

ITALIAN

FINNISH

NORWEGIAN